the tiny book of
TIME

Creating time for the things that matter

KIM PICKIN and
NICKY SINGER

D1136856

First published in 1999
by HEADLINE BOOK PUBLISHING

10 9 8 7 6 5 4 3 2

ISBN 0 7472 6244 6

Designed and typeset by Ben Cracknell Studios

Printed and bound in France by Brodard & Taupin

HEADLINE BOOK PUBLISHING
A division of Hodder Headline PLC
338 Euston Road
London NW1 3BH

We all used to have time. Before snail mail became fax became e-mail. Before we aspired to perfect jobs, perfect relationships and perfect homes. Before we had children.

The Tiny Book of Time is about recapturing time. On each page is a big idea or a practical tip to help you streamline the jobs you **must** do and achieve the things you really **want** to.

Because you can regain control. Not by cramming more into your day.

But by changing how you think.

Contents

~

The book is divided into eight sections:

Wisdom

~

Work

~

Home

~

Friends & Family

~

High Days & Holidays

~

Children

~

Partner

~

Yourself

Wisdom

~

Before you start a task,
ask yourself three questions:

~ Does it *have* to be done?

~ Do *I* have to do it?

~ Do I have to do it *now*?

Don't wait until you've finished to have fun.
You may never finish.

A big **task** is just a lot of little tasks
waiting to get out.

Pick 'em off one at a time.

When an opportunity comes up – from an
expedition to a training course – ask yourself
not just 'Do I want to do this?' but 'Is *now*
the right time?'

Wisdom

~

If life collapses around you – your
relationship fails, you lose your job, your
child is seriously ill – decide as early as
possible what you can and cannot influence.

Channel your energies into the former.

Know yourself. Maybe you're an
adrenaline junkie. Are you so used to being
overcommitted that, as soon as you spot a
gap in your schedule, you fill it?

Don't.

Wisdom

~

You could always pretend to be out.

Break down the mental barriers between
work and leisure.

If you *have* to do something, try thinking of
ways to make it more enjoyable.

You don't need to go places just because
there are aeroplanes.

In all areas of your life, consume less – and
spend more time digesting.

Wisdom
~

Take time to save time.

~ Put Christmas card addresses on disk.

~ Construct an **indoor** camp of chairs
and blankets for your children
before starting **that** vital chore.

~ Spend an hour **figuring** out how to get
your computer **to do** things that
would take **you even** longer.

Don't do everyone else's thinking
for them.

Their brains will shrivel – and yours may
explode.

Wisdom

~

If you wait until you can get it done
perfectly it may never get done.

~

And if you wait until you can afford
the one you want, it may be too late
to enjoy it.

Fallow time isn't wasted time.

Allowing the earth to rest ensures a
better harvest.

Wisdom

~

How much time do you waste searching
for and rewriting your 'To Do' lists?
Co-ordinate *everything* you need to do –
from rearranging a meeting to replacing the
boiler – in one large spiral-bound notebook.

And if you keep small spiral notebooks by
each phone, you'll be surprised how many
messages used to go astray.

Wisdom

~

If you radiate efficiency, others are
less likely to help.

Leave space for them to make a
genuine contribution.

What would you do in a perfect world?
Can you make even a tiny part of that
dream come true?

Today?

If you're agonising, ask yourself 'Is
this decision particularly hard to
make because the options are actually
equally good or bad?'

If they are, it doesn't matter
which you choose.

Wisdom

~

You don't have to see everything and know
all about everything – not even
'the news'.

Trust that you will find out what
you need to know.

Practise saying: 'Thank you. No.'

Wisdom

~

Sometimes actually doing something,
such as ringing the plumber or gluing a vase,
takes less time than relisting it 'to do' for
the fifth time.

Just do it.

Make friends with delay.

A wait at the doctors is a chance to read a book. Even a traffic jam can be a gift of time – to think through that letter or list.

Wisdom

~

You can't progress on all fronts at once.

Maybe this phase of your life is
about building your career, the next about
enjoying your family. And *then* you
can create a perfect home.

Fast forward to your deathbed.

What do you wish you'd spent
more time doing?

If you want something done, encourage
someone else to think it was their idea.

Just because a request **is** reasonable doesn't
mean you have **to** comply with it.

Wisdom

~

Spot life's synergies.

- Find a work project you can do with a friend.

- Let the kids cycle beside you as you jog.

- Extend your business trip into a romantic weekend with your partner.

- Build a garden shed with your dad.

Stop filing before it starts.

If you decide who's going to keep
the master and where it's going to
be kept, then everyone else can
throw their copies away.

Distinguish between the urgency of
the task and that of the task-setter.

Go with the task.

Know when to shine.
Not every job needs to be done perfectly.

Some just need to be done.

Tackle useless paperwork at source.

Review circulation lists regularly to halt
those reports, printouts and journals that
you never read but feel you should.

Build in five minutes at the end of each
day to organise your mind and your desk
for the following day.

You'll get tomorrow off to a better start.

Work
~

Get smart about keeping up to date.

- Learn to skim-read.

- Split the reading with a colleague and brief each other.

- Subscribe to a précis service.

- Or relax. You'll probably get to hear the most important stuff anyway.

Work

~

Just because it's a fax or an e-mail
doesn't mean you have to stop what
you are doing.

Resist the tyranny of modern
communications.

Delegate more than you think
your deputy is capable of.

He or she will probably
rise to the occasion.

Work

Talk less.

Why is it that we fix routine meetings for the morning when many of us are at our most productive?

Do tough work in the morning. Save your weariest hours for phonecalls, filing – and those routine meetings.

If your boss gives you one task
too many, ask what you should
drop instead.

Perfect the art of writing briefly.

Crisp, short memos and reports win respect
and admiration – especially from
hard-pressed senior people.

Work

~

If you're having trouble getting started, tell yourself you're only going to do ten minutes' worth.

If it goes well – and it usually does – stick with it. If not, try ten minutes at another time.

There comes a point when you must stop
collecting data and make that decision.

Trust your instincts. They're usually better
than you think.

Work

~

Parkinson's Law still holds. Work expands to fill the time available. So ... contain the available time.

Don't stay late. And don't start too far ahead of the deadline.

Work

~

Avoid writing those old-fashioned and
time-consuming minutes.

1.1 Instead, write an agreed action
list as the meeting progresses.

1.2 Photocopy and circulate
it as people leave.

It'll make for sharper decisions and
prompter action.

Learn to wait.

Situations often improve just with
the passage of time.

Work

~

Wherever possible, scribble your
reply directly onto incoming memos
or mail, and return them to the sender.
Only make copies when you *must*
have a record.

Always remember that doing nothing
is a genuine option.

If you grasp every opportunity you'll spread
yourself – or your organisation – too thin.

Work

~

Give yourself time to concentrate. Put a sign on your desk or door to tell your colleagues you can't be interrupted for an hour or two. They'll respect this if you're otherwise available.

They may even follow suit.

It's worth spending a day training someone
how to do a task that takes
you an hour.

Otherwise you'll never shed it.

Home

~

You don't have to do things
the way your mother did.

In fact you may not have
to do them at all.

Home

~

You can't expect a busy home to
be tidy all the time.

Set your sights on once a week.

Train the people you live with that
items piled at the bottom of the stairs are
supposed to be on their way up.

Caring for things you
care about isn't a chore.

Get rid of the things you don't care about,
and care for those you do.

Start your photograph
album from today.

If you try to do the backlog
first, you'll never arrive at today.

Home

~

Are your old cheque stubs in the top drawer
of your desk and your envelopes on the other
side of the room?

Keep things you use hourly at your elbow,
daily within easy reach, monthly in
cupboards, and less often than that in your
attic – or someone else's.

When clearing out ask not 'Is this usable?'
but 'Do I use it?'

Possessions devour time.

Before bringing anything new into
your home ask yourself, 'Do I want
this enough to dust, polish, sort,
insure, search behind, walk around
and trip over it?'

Wrap clingfilm around a wet paintbrush. It saves cleaning it if you're planning to do more decorating the next day.

Face it. If it's been in pieces for six months,
you can live without it.

~

It is possible to spring-clean the kitchen.

Just take it a drawer at a time.

Try the new supermarket delivery
services for your toilet paper, coffee
and other staples.

You can still go to the store to
sniff the melons – if you want to.

Phone ahead or phone instead.

Shop assistants generally answer the
phone before they serve the queue
at the counter.

~

Don't return product registration cards.
They don't affect your guarantee and do
generate junk mail. Just keep your receipt
as proof of purchase.

~

Not interested in double-glazing?
Some phone companies can screen out sales
calls for you. Inquire.

Home

~

Have you ever asked yourself why you open
junk mail before you throw it away?

~

Some time-savers don't. Think twice before
paying your bills by direct debit. They're a
nightmare to unscramble if you – or they –
lose track of your money.

Combat the notion of 'the best' –
it belongs to the advertisers.

Actually any one of six bathroom taps is
probably beautiful and functional enough.
Why not just choose the first one you like?

You gain half a day at the weekend if you foodshop midweek.

Midweek doesn't seem to notice.

Simplify.

A perfect peach is as delectable
as peach pie.

Convenience food is improving all the time.
Don't feel guilty about eating it – or serving
it to guests.

If you need to prepare packed lunches, you can make and freeze sandwiches a week at a time. Pick them out each morning and they'll defrost by lunchtime.

Note: not recommended for lettuce or mayo.

Home
~

Despite all our labour-saving appliances we spend as long on laundry as our grandmothers did.

Don't feel you have to wash every once-worn item, just because you can.

Home

~

What's so special about uniform grass?
Nature obviously has other plans for your
lawn. Is it time to welcome
those daisies?

~

Design a garden that offers you
pleasure, not forced labour. If you like
staking, tying and deadheading – fine.
If not, choose shrubs.

Home

~

Plant alpines. And anything else
that's forgiving about water.

~

Forget houseplants.
At least the living kind.

Don't invest time in people you know
will never become real friends.

Your real friends don't get
enough of you as it is.

Try building ageing relatives into your real life, not just into best-behaviour teas. You're more likely to invite them if they can contribute to some family project – like sorting the photos.

And it may be more fun for them.

Appropriate a feast day. Holding an annual gathering – Midsummer's Eve, Hallowe'en – is an efficient as well as delightful way of building traditions and nurturing your friends as a group.

And it's much less work than ten dinner parties.

An unexpected pleasure often
lingers longer.

If the chance arises, drop in on a friend –
even if only for ten minutes.

When the family visit, it's their job to do things your way – not *vice versa.*

Don't underestimate the impact
of place on time.

An hour's conversation in a hotel lounge
may be worth three in a noisy bar. Hotel
lounges are comfortable (especially for
women alone), surprisingly cheap and
the staff never hassle you.

More time with your friends or
relatives isn't necessarily better.

Some relationships work best on an
occasional basis.

Friends & Family

~

Arrange to meet your siblings without their
partners. Not because you don't like their
partners but because your time together
will be different.

~

Similarly, feel good about seeing
your parents one to one. Even grown-ups
need time alone with just their
mother – or father.

People who don't volunteer to help
when they visit you should only be seen in
their own homes.

Better two lines on a postcard than a longer
letter never sent.

Skip fancy dinners in favour of Saturday tea
or Sunday brunch.

It's your company not your cooking
that your friends care about.

Allow younger siblings to grow up. Once
they pass eighteen they can fix their own
punctures and organise their own finances –
just like you did.

Face up to it. All your friends are frantic too. What's wrong with booking six months ahead?

Or try setting up 'default' arrangements. If you always meet on the first Tuesday of the month, no one has to co-ordinate diaries and it's much more likely to happen.

Give gifts to your godchildren not on their birthday but on yours. That way you won't forget – and they'll enjoy an unexpected present.

Design a Christmas that won't make you cross. If that means sausage and beans rather than turkey and stress, so be it.

And don't forget to schedule in some recovery time. Don't book Christmas up completely.

You don't have to have done everything
before the guests arrive.

Sometimes it's nicer for you – and them – if
they can help to create the occasion.

Don't beat yourself up if you didn't get to
make the cranberry sauce.

Protect your right to have done enough –
if not everything.

Re-think gifts, big time.

- Better just the right gift when you happen
  upon it, than an annual piece of junk.

- Favour presents that don't need dusting:
  a massage, a baby-sit, a subscription.

- Enter 'no-present' pacts. If you use
  Christmas just to be together, you're
  giving the most precious gift of all – time.

WHY BE SO HUNG UP...

For children's parties: encourage your circle
of friends to give – and ask for – a specified
(small) amount of money. It'll make
everyone's lives easier and the child may
prefer one really great present to twenty
bits of plastic.

...ABOUT GIVING CASH?

For weddings: most couples already have a toaster. Could you donate to something large that they haven't got?

And christenings: when he's eighteen your godson may prefer to see how his savings nest-egg has grown rather than polish his third silver tankard.

It's tempting to plan new and exciting
holiday experiences.

But remember you may really need *less*
not more stimulation.

High Days & Holidays

~

Write and re-use packing lists. One for
summer and one for winter.

~

Challenge yourself to pack less each time
you go away. It's surprising how inventive
you can be if something's missing.

~

If you travel a lot keep a duplicate washbag
of toiletries ready to go.

Let your standards take a holiday too.

Limit holiday postcards to
five words, or one joke.

Or simply don't send them.

Consider a holiday house swap with
like-minded friends. You don't have to pack
towels, travel cots, kitchen knives –
or even food.

The effort of going away on
Friday night is worth it. A three-day
weekend seems twice as long as
a two-day weekend.

Children

~

Raising children is not a tick-box project and days often go by without any obvious achievements.

Trust that you have spent your time well just by being there.

Children

~

Expose your child to time management.

Allow her to be late occasionally and suffer
the consequences. Maybe she'll start
nagging you to get to school.

Your baby doesn't care if her
clothes aren't ironed.

Nor does she mind coming on the school run
in her pyjamas.

Children

~

A toddler's obstructiveness increases in inverse proportion to the time remaining.

Try to get him dressed before he senses your rush.

Children
~

Your children probably grew up since
you last looked – maybe they can set
the table now?

Note: your expectations may in any
case be too low. Your six-year-old can
vacuum, your eight-year-old can sew on
a button and your ten-year-old can supervise
the reading of a younger child.

Children

~

Forget the videocam. Just sit in
the front row of the nativity play
and gaze at your child king.

A memory doesn't need preparation,
doesn't take up shelf space and lasts forever.
And it's possible you'll see something the
lens can't capture.

Children

~

Stick a school checklist by the front door.

Encourage your child to check for himself whether he has his recorder, football boots and library book.

Children

~

Have two: a hairbrush upstairs
and downstairs, ditto a toothbrush
and toothpaste.

It's a very small investment for a big pay-off
in avoiding pre-school trauma.

Allot specific and accessible places
for things your child uses regularly.
That way he can find and reach
things for himself.

Children
~

Leave a toy or game on the kitchen table
before your child returns from school.
If you don't mention it (and this is crucial),
she'll probably play with it rather than pick
a fight with her sister.

MORE TOYS...

Too much choice paralyses your child. And unused toys are just clutter for you.

- Give ninety of the wax crayons to a local play group.

- Take toys out of circulation. You can re-introduce these 'new' things in a holiday 'anti-boredom box'.

...LESS TIME

- Pay your children nominal sums for toys they will never use. Or get them to set up stall in the front garden. They can then save for something they really want or need.

- Remember *before* their birthdays that less is more. And remind grandma.

Children

~

Don't try to pack in too much when
you take your kids out for the day. You'll
get ragged and they won't
enjoy themselves.

~

Likewise, think twice about after-school
activities. Evenings without grief might do
you all more good than learning to ice-skate,
play the flute or tie a reef knot.

Children

~

It's tempting to tidy up after children because it's quicker that way. But only in the short term. If your current repertoire of incentives and threats doesn't work, try putting it in writing...

'Dear children. One day scientists will invent socks that put themselves in the laundry basket. Meanwhile, can you help?'

Children

~

One way to have regular time alone
with each child is to devise a task – going
to the dump, watering the plants – that you
only do with them. It'll also make that
job special.

Children

~

Stop doing the children's
thinking for them.

If you always insist they wear a
sweater how will they discover cold and
decide they need to remember one?

ON NAMING ITEMS

- Invest in a laundry marker.
  Nametape only *in extremis*.

- For socks loop the tape and sew across the
  end rather than all the way round.

- Use different coloured nametapes for
  each child so you can distinguish grey
  school socks at a glance.

Children

~

Re-think your social life.

Try taking the children to a friend's house for a 'video night'. Feed them first and then let them goggle while you eat. This way you get some quality adult time, save on baby-sitting and still get home by 9pm.

Children

~

Instead of dragging the kids into
town to buy their present for Daddy, why
not encourage them to make a cheque
promising to 'pay the bearer one tidy room,
one clean car or one breakfast in bed' – to be
redeemed on request?

Quality time for children is when they need
it, not necessarily when you want to give it.

For the teenager this may be four
in the morning.

Children

~

If your teenager eats all the food in the house, give him the weekly budget and get him to do the shopping.

Children

~

When your daughter is at college, or
abroad, you have no idea where she is each
night. Yet you still wait up for her
when she comes home.

Why?

Try to go to bed at the
same time as each other.

At least occasionally.

Partner

~

Arrange to meet your partner in unfamiliar
surroundings.

It's possible the person you fell in love with
will turn up.

Partner

~

Most women think most men don't do their fair share in the home. Try chore-swapping for a few weeks. You may be able to right the balance – a little.

You may also discover that you'd prefer to do all the ironing rather than clean dog-mess off shoes.

Partner

~

Accept that you can never radically
alter someone else's relationship with time.

Your partner's punctuality
(or lack of it) is as much part of
them as the colour of their eyes.

Partner

~

If you get to the point where you need time
apart, take it.

It's as likely to save your relationship
as to end it.

Partner

~

'You know I always wanted to be a farmer.'
'What? You never mentioned it.'

Don't forget to dovetail your dreams. Share
life plans with each other while there's still
time to make them happen.

Businesses often take their managers away
for the day to make long-term plans and
crunch decisions.

Why not do the same with your most
important life colleague?

Partner

~

Give yourself and your partner time to decelerate after work.

If you're moving at different speeds, friction is inevitable.

Partner

~

Share weekend plans in advance – otherwise
you'll discover, just too late, that your
partner's planning to do their tax in the slot
you've earmarked to choose paint together.

If your partner fritters away
hard-earned free time, accept that's his or
her prerogative – so long as you get an equal
amount of time to spend as you wish.

Partner

~

You don't have to go to a party just because your partner is going.

Hearing about a party you didn't go to is more fun than being there when you felt like a night in.

Partner

~

If you want help, ask for it.

If you want it again, don't criticise how the
job was done the first time.

Partner

~

Beware the laundry trap.

If your partner's washing becomes your responsibility your work will be taken for granted. If it remains theirs – but you will do it if asked – they still have to do the thinking and may even appreciate your help.

Partner

~

Sometimes time alone in your
own home to do your own thing is
better than a holiday.

Invite your partner and/or children to
go and visit friends for a weekend.

Partner

~

If one of you works outside the home
and the other in it, you may need different
things from your holiday time.

Discuss?

Yourself

~

Pause. Have you been so busy just getting through the days that you've lost sight of your deeper goals?

Take another look. Notice what makes you happy and try to build more of it into your life.

Knowing what you want is half way to making it happen.

Yourself

~

Avoid anything that makes you,
your relationships or your home
feel inadequate.

Magazines, advertisements, catalogues and
shop windows are *designed* to fuel
dissatisfaction.

Get more sleep.

Mountains never take so long to climb when
you're rested.

Walk when you can.

That way you get to think, exercise –
and arrive somewhere.

The perfect outfit isn't in the one
clothes shop you haven't visited.

Confine yourself to the four shops
where you are normally most
successful and then stop.

If you keep saying 'yes' to everyone else,
you are saying 'no' to yourself.

Try a whole week without watching
TV, then balance what you missed –
and gained.

Yourself

~

There is never a right time to have a child.

When planning a family, don't think about what age you want to be when you have your first child, but how old you'll be when you have your last.

Then add thirty years and see how old you'll be when you get to play with that child's child.

Practise the art of shutting
people up politely.

You are not obliged to listen
to leaking taps.

Indecision eats time. Sometimes it's actually easier to decide – and deal with the consequences – than to keep dithering.

~

Anger eats time. If you can change the situation, go ahead. If you can't, try changing the way you look at it.

Yourself

~

Worry eats time.
Download with a friend.

~

Regret eats time. There is *nothing*
you can do to change the past.

Be generous with your praise.

It can be a great motivator.

Yourself

~

Don't soldier on. Go to bed.
See a doctor. Take a pill.

The sooner you collapse, the
earlier you'll recover.

Let someone else take the lead.

It won't be the occasion you would have
organised. It could even be better.

Yourself

~

Are you considering turning down
a career opportunity to spend more time with
your family?

It may seem like a wrench – now – but
remember, in a year's time your priorities
will probably have shifted so much that you
wouldn't take the job even if you
were offered it.

Yourself

~

If you made an appointment at a
beauty salon, you'd keep it. Why not book
an hour with yourself in the bathroom
each week?

A face-pack, manicure or perfumed
bath will do much more for your sense of
well-being than another evening in front of
the television.

Yourself

~

If you're going to say 'no', do it as soon and
as clearly as possible.

Constantly leaving doors ajar stops
you concentrating on the things you
do intend to do.

You don't always have to do
two things at once.

If you were given one car to last your entire
lifetime, you'd look after it. What are you
doing about your body?

You will function better in all departments
of your life if you allocate guilt-free time to
body maintenance.

Let there be silence.

Don't always be the first to volunteer.

Yourself

~

The person whose job it is to
make time for you is you.

About the Authors

~

Kim Pickin is a business consultant, advertising copywriter and compulsive list-maker. She works from home, alternating between devising marketing campaigns for large companies and caring for three small children and their pet chicken.

Nicky Singer is a novelist, TV presenter, wife and mother of three. But not necessarily in that order. Her latest novel, *My Mother's Daughter*, is about surrogacy and her latest child, a daughter, is about to sleep through the night.

E-mail them on createtime@hotmail.com